AUG 06

KN

COOL careers

for girls

with Animals

COOL careers

for
girls

with

Animals

Ceel Pasternak & Linda Thornburg

Impact Publications

Liability/Warranty: The authors and publisher have made every attempt to provide the reader with accurate information. However, given constant changes in the employment field, they make no claims that this information will remain accurate at the time of reading. Furthermore, this information is presented for information purposes only. The authors and publisher make no claims that using this information will guarantee the reader a job. The authors and publisher shall not be liable for any loss or damages incurred in the process of following the advice presented in this book.

Library of Congress Cataloging-in-Publication Data

Pasternak, Ceel, 1932-
    Cool careers for girls with animals / Ceel Pasternak & Linda Thornburg.
      p. cm.
    Includes bibliographical references and index.
    Summary: Profiles ten women who work with animals, in such jobs as horse farm owner, veterinarian, and exotic animal trainer, and explains their duties and how they prepared for and got their positions.
    ISBN 1-57023-108-7 (hardcover)—ISBN 1-57023-105-2 (softcover)
    1. Women animal specialists—Vocational guidance—Juvenile literature. 2. Animal specialists—Vocational guidance—Juvenile literature. 3. Animal Culture—Vocational guidance—Juvenile literature. 4. Women animal specialists—Biography—Juvenile literature. 5. Animal specialists—Biography—Juvenile literature. [1. Women animal specialists—Vocational guidance. 2. Animal specialists—vocational guidance. 3. Animal culture—vocational guidance. 4. Vocational guidance. 5. Occupations.]
    I. Thornburg, Linda,
    1949- . II. Title.
SF80.P281998
636'.0023—dc21   98-48086
                      CIP
                      AC

Publisher: For information on Impact Publications, including current and forthcoming publications, authors, press kits, bookstore, and submission requirements, visit Impact's Web site: www.impactpublications.com

Publicity/Rights: For information on publicity, author interviews, and subsidiary rights, contact the Public Relations and Marketing Department: Tel. 703/361-7300 or Fax 703/335-9486.

Sales/Distribution: All paperback bookstore sales are handled through Impact's trade distributor: National Book Network, 15200 NBN Way, Blue Ridge Summit, PA 17214, Tel. 1-800-462-6420. All other sales and distribution inquiries should be directed to the publisher: Sales Department, IMPACT PUBLICATIONS, 9104-N Manassas Dr., Manassas Park, VA 20111-5211, Tel. 703/361-7300, Fax 703/335-9486, or E-mail: coolcareers@impactpublications.com

Dedicated to the women in this
book who were kind enough to share
their experiences with us in order to
help girls.

Contents

Careers with Animals

If you love animals, you should consider working with animals as a possible career choice. Not only are there many animals you might work with, from dogs and cats to chimpanzees, but there are many types of work. You could do research outdoors or in a laboratory, you could care for animals, you could train them, you could raise animals, or you could treat them like a doctor does. You could work with a group that wants to protect endangered species. You could work for someone else or for yourself, you could be in a city or in the country, and you could travel or just stay in one place.

To help you explore working with animals, we've profiled 10 women in different jobs who love their work. You'll learn the duties and responsibilities that go with the job title, but you'll also learn about the women themselves—what drew them to their work, how they found their first job, and how they took advantage of the opportunities presented to them.

These women continue to learn every day.

All the women whose stories you'll read in this book love animals unconditionally. Many of the jobs require good communications skills and a flair for showmanship. They all take hard work and patience, and most of them require a deep understanding of animals. You'll read about women in jobs as diverse as wildlife manager, exotic animal trainer, and zookeeper, and you'll learn about women who own their own businesses.

We all want to do work we enjoy and to make a good living at it. Deciding on a career is a big step, usually made up of a lot of small decisions. Your career path will no doubt take many turns as you follow your talents, interests, and opportunities. Because your future includes more than work, you need to think about lifestyle choices, and how these will complement the type of work you do. So we've shown you how 10 women handle their personal lives, along with their work lives.

How To Use This Book

If you are wondering how to get a job working with animals, this book is a good place to start. After you read each woman's story, you'll find a checklist with some clues about what type of person would be good in the particular job profiled. We've included some information about what salary you might expect to earn in jobs similar to those described. Look for the sources for the information included here and check them periodically to find the latest information.

Getting Started Now

The final chapter, Getting Started on Your Own Career Path, suggests books to read and organizations that will help with more information. Many groups have both college student chapters and local chapters, which you may want to join to keep up with trends and changes. Some groups have a mentor program. Finding someone who will take you under her or his wing and be there to answer questions you have can help you decide what you should be doing now to prepare for a career with animals. The professional groups cited in the final chapter are also possible sources for scholarships.

It's not too early to begin thinking about what work you would like to do as an adult. The earlier you identify the work you want, the earlier you can start preparing for a career. That includes taking the right courses in school now. And if you're interested in working with animals, don't be afraid to volunteer to help out at a park, with a veterinarian, at an animal shelter, or with an environmental organization. Check with your local zoo or aquarium for volunteer opportunities or internships.

We hope you enjoy the stories in this book. Look for our books on other careers as you begin thinking about what type of work might be right for you.

COOL careers
for girls
with Animals

Dee Craig

VETERINARIAN, LAS CRUCES, NM

Pre-veterinary coursework, Doctor of Veterinary Medicine

Small Animal
Veterinarian

Dr Dee's Dumb Friends

The thing Dee Craig likes best about her job is when she can diagnose an animal's illness. The thing she likes least is when she can't. Dee is a small animal veterinarian. She treats dogs and cats, reptiles, birds, rabbits, rats and mice, and other "pocket pets."

Dee is a general practitioner who owns her own practice. That means she will treat whatever animals are brought in by their owners. But she doesn't treat large animals such as livestock or horses.

To be a good vet, Dee says, you have to be able to get along with people. It's even more important than getting along with the animals. When a pet owner tells Dee what problem the animal has, Dee has to interpret this information so she can diagnose the problem or illness correctly. For example, if the owner says a pet dog is always itching, Dee has to find out where the itch is, what might be caus-

- Vet technicians accredited $18,500 to $40,000
- Doctors of veterinary medicine (DVM)- average government $54,400
- Average DVM practice owner $79,600
- Average DVM practice employee $38,700

Source: Encyclopedia of Careers and Vocational Guidance

ing it, and what "always" really means. Then she can recommend the treatment that will best solve the problem.

"Owners fall into one of three categories," she says. "First, there is the owner who treats the pet like a member of the family and will do anything possible to make sure the animal is healthy and comfortable. Then there is the practical owner who loves the pet, but won't spend outrageous amounts of money to save the animal. And finally, there is the person whose animal just lives in the backyard and doesn't get paid any attention except when he's sick." Dee has to decide which type of owner she is dealing with and then recommend the treatment that is right for the pet, but also right for the owner.

"Vets have different styles," she says. "My style is to be pretty frank with the owner and to try to explain what's really going on in terms the owner can understand. Other vets have different styles. Eventually, owners find the vets who suit their personalities. That's why it's just as important to deal well with people as it is to be able to diagnose and treat animals. If you have the medical knowledge but not the people skills, you won't do very well as a general practitioner. You would be better off in research."

Captured by the Challenges

Dee did not own her own pet until the 7th grade, when she got a dog who became a good buddy. But it wasn't the animals that really attracted her to veterinary medicine. It was the challenge of solving the puzzle of what was making an animal sick.

As a girl, Dee was always near or at the top of her class in school. She was smart, and she thrived on intellectual challenges. Her father was a sergeant in the Army, so Dee's family

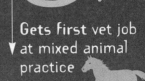
moved several times. She lived in Colorado Springs, CO; in Waynesville, MO; and in Wahiawa, HI. As a military kid she became independent pretty fast, and learned to make friends and fit in wherever she was. But in Hawaii, she had the worst time. Her mother is Hawaiian, and her father is from the Philippines. "In Hawaii, they didn't know how to treat me," Dee says. "I looked like a native but I talked like a mainlander."

Her father was stationed at Fort Leonard Wood in Missouri from the time she was in 7th grade on. Dee went to junior high on the Army base and to high school in Waynesville, MO, just a few miles from the base. It was her 10th grade biology teacher, Mr. Noe, who got her interested in veterinary medicine. "Our biology labs were just like college labs," Dee says. "We dissected animals and learned about the different organs. Mr. Noe asked me what I was going to do with my life when he saw I was good in biology. I said I didn't know, and

he suggested being a vet. Where can I learn about that? I asked. He got me a job with a vet during the summer and from then on I was hooked. I was fascinated with the challenges of diagnosing the illness and with doing the surgery."

Dee is one of four children, the second oldest, behind a brother. Then came another brother and a sister, who is 7 years younger than she is. Her parents never told her to get good grades. They didn't need to. It was just expected. One time Dee came home with a B+ and her parents asked her what had gone wrong.

Dee graduated valedictorian of her high school class. Because of that, she got a complete scholarship to the University of Missouri at Columbia. She knew she wanted to be a veterinarian so she took the pre-vet core courses she had to have to get into vet school—biology, physics, mathematics, and physiology. She thought if she didn't make it into vet

Moves to Las Cruces

Opens own practice

There are lots of jobs in the veterinary field.
You could be in health inspecting meat plants and slaughter houses, in research for the medicine and pet food industries or for pharmaceutical and drug industries.

school, she could use the same core courses to go into bioengineering. "It's always good to have a plan to fall back on in case you don't get into the graduate school you want," she says.

To give her money for room and board and books as an undergraduate, she worked as a server and then assistant manager at a McDonalds. She finished her core courses and applied to vet school as a junior. She got accepted to the 4-year program, skipping her last year of college. Her grade point was 3.9.

"I didn't really expect to get accepted," she says. "I was just applying for practice."

In veterinary college she met her future husband, Maury, who worked as the farm manager at the university's Equine Center. They got married after Dee's 2nd year in veterinary college.

You also could specialize in veterinary opthamology or pathology or work in a zoo or animal park. Now many schools encourage you to specialize in one type of veterinary medicine early on.

GROUNDBREAKERS

Jane Goodall, in 1966, established a research camp in a national park in Tanzania where she studied chimpanzee behavior for 15 years. She has written several books about chimps, the animal similar in many ways to humans.

In 1977 she founded the Jane Goodall Institute, which is committed to wildlife research, environmental education and conservation, and the welfare of animals, especially chimpanzees.

For more information, contact the Jane Goodall Institute, P.O. Box 14890, Silver Spring, MD 20911-4890. (301) 565-0086.

Vet School Is Hard Work

Veterinary school turned out to be harder than her undergraduate work, and Dee had to give up her job at McDonalds so she could study more. But she got loans from the school to supplement her scholarships. "I never took a dime from my parents as a college student," she says. "In fact, once I sent money home when my parents needed it. A father who has four children to support on the Army staff sergeant's salary can't afford to send his kids to college. But this didn't keep me from going. I knew there was a way to do it and I did it."

In Dee's class 22 out of 76 students were female. "We all knew we could become vets and still be feminine," she says. "We knew we were as good as the guys."

The first 2 years of vet school Dee learned the medicine. The third and fourth year she got to practice it. One of her most memorable moments was when she had to palpate a ewe (stick her arm inside the ewe). The ewe was about ready to give birth, and Dee helped to deliver two twin lambs. "Here I was, this little person, and I pulled those lambs out," she says. "These big, husky guys just stood around and watched, wishing they could have been the ones to do it."

Dee thought about going into horse medicine, but she wasn't tall enough. "Besides," she says, "I didn't grow up on a farm or around livestock, and I didn't really know the culture of people who raise livestock. It was easier to go into small animal veterinary medicine."

Dee studied hard in veterinary school. She got up at 6:30, was in class from 7:30 through 5:00 p.m., and then studied every night from 5:00 until about 9 or 9:30. After that she took an hour for recreation or fun, often playing volleyball with friends.

When she graduated as a doctor of veterinary medicine, she got a job in a town near Waynesville with a veterinarian who treated both livestock and small animals. Dr. Barnett, the vet who hired her, was a "classic good guy," Dee says. He was there when she needed him, but he didn't hover over her. In fact, he was out seeing to livestock, and if she wanted advice, she had to call him. Dee learned how to order medicine and supplies and pretty much run the small animal practice by working with Dr. Barnett.

Two years later Dee's husband, Maury, returned from a trip to New Mexico with tales

CAREER CHECKLIST ✓

This career is for you if you ...

- Like to solve puzzles and problems

- Can see the forest for the trees

- Love science and math and have excellent study habits

- Get along well with people

- Can work by yourself and aren't afraid of hard work

of how great the state was. He convinced Dee that they should move, so the couple packed up and headed to the Southwest. Maury wanted to study veterinary entomology and New

more than in Missouri. She didn't have trouble finding people who wanted to hire her for their veterinary practices, but she did run into a problem. In New Mexico, you have to take

Vet school is expensive, but even if your parents don't have money, you can get in. I knew good grades would get me into college. Many states will waive the tuition for college if you graduate high enough in your high school class.

Mexico State University in Las Cruces had a good program.

Dee liked her new home state immediately; the people were friendly and the sun shone

the state boards before you can practice veterinary medicine. They weren't giving them for about 6 months. So Dee found a doctor in El Paso, just a few miles across the Texas border

Then there are private
scholarships and grants.
Get on the Internet and
mention your GPA.
See what you can find.
Don't just rely on the
university system.
There is money
available if you
have the tenacity to find it.

from the town of Las Cruces, who needed an assistant. Dr. McCabe hired Dee as a technician. A technician can do almost anything a veterinarian does except diagnose and prescribe medication. Dr. McCabe agreed to pay her the same as he would a technician while she waited to take the state boards. She took blood, gave x-rays, and even cleaned the animal cages. Eventually, after she had taken and passed her boards, she ran a small animal clinic for the doctor.

Her Own Practice

Then Dee decided she wanted to work for herself. But to build her own practice was prohibitively expensive. She would need the land and a building, which she just could not afford. So she found a doctor who was retiring and bought his small animal practice. Because banks don't easily loan money to veterinarians who buy another doctor's practice, the retiring doctor financed the sale of his practice to her. She hopes to do the same with another veterinarian when she retires.

Her husband Maury is 10 years older than Dee, so Dee would like to retire at 55—in about 15 years—so the couple can travel. She would like to take a cruise around the world. She has to look for an associate for her practice before then—someone who will be good to work with and will want to buy the practice from her when she is ready to sell it.

In the near future, Dee plans to expand by doing some behavioral consulting. She will go to the homes of pet owners and suggest ways to change undesirable animal behavior. "It's all dependent on whether or not the owner can follow through with the information they get," she says. "Sometimes that's hard to do."

In a bigger town than Las Cruces (70,000) she would have competition from specialists who are board certified in behavioral consulting. But there are no specialists in the area, so she can offer this service. However, she can't call herself an expert in behavioral consultation. Only vets who have actually studied that in school can do that.

Dee goes to lots of seminars and conferences to learn about behavioral consulting, and about how to treat animals she might not be as familiar with, such as some of the reptiles her clients bring in. That's a good way to keep learning, she says. She also sometimes consults with other vets, if there is a problem she can't solve.

Running a veterinary practice is a demanding job. Dee has to oversee the ordering of all the supplies and medicines, develop new clients, supervise her staff, and care for the animals. She needs lots of energy to do that. To help keep fit, she works out at the gym. She recently discovered karate, which she also uses to keep fit and to develop focus. For relaxation, she "crafts." She makes porcelain dolls and Christmas tree skirts and other gifts for friends and relatives. She also loves to read science fiction. Recently, she and Maury were able to build their dream house high on a hill in Las Cruces.

Daniela Spigai

CO OWNER, PRIVILEGED PETS, ALEXANDRIA, VA

Graduate Fashion Institute of Technology

Entrepreneur
Pet Sitter & Exerciser

Substitute Parent for Pampered Pets

Daniela used to walk dogs and take care of neighbors' pets when she was a girl. Now she and her husband, Steve, own a pet care business. With more than 200 customers, Daniela, Steve, and her 5 employees visit about 65 houses a day, mostly for midday walks. They are also busy on weekends and holidays. "In this business you need to be available when others need you most, and you need to understand it will take lots of time. That's why you have to love doing it. I haven't had a full day off in a year."

"This is a full-service, pet-walking, and overnight-care business," says Daniela. "Most of our service is afternoon and midday walks for working people or someone out of town for the day. We do morning and evening visits, trips to the vet and groomer, and we pick up and drop off at trainers."

- Single person by themselves - $30,000 to $45,000 per year
- Two people $60,000 to $90,000 per year
- Larger business well over $100,000 per year

Attends Fashion Institute in New York

Meets Steve

Joins Nordstrom department store

Daniela also administers medicines, and gives injections. For example, cats often have diabetes and need insulin shots, urine tests, and a call to tell the vet how the pet is doing.

One of Daniela's favorite things is walking dogs who do not have to be leashed. She takes several at a time to a local area near the Potomac River where she lets the dogs run and plays with them. "Animals need that social interaction," she says.

Daniela enjoys working with clients who really love their pets. "The pets treat me like a member of the family. As the business grows, it is hard for me to turn one of 'my' pets over to an employee. Customers want me to be the person caring for their pet, and I want to know how the animal is doing, so usually I arrange to see it at least once a week."

When Daniela and Steve bought the business 5 years ago, Privileged Pets had a small number of customers. It grew 114 percent the first year, mostly by word of mouth, and about 44 percent each year since. Handling the paperwork and telephones and scheduling takes from 4 to 6 hours a day, says Daniela. "We also give advice to our customers over the telephone, especially if there is a new puppy." She gets help from her sister, a close friend, Steve, and other employees.

From Elvis the Pig to Pet Turtles

Daniela's customers have all kinds of pets. "When a new client calls I want to be sure we can take good care of the pet. I analyze what the customer really wants us to do and I rely on my instincts and experience. For example, I will turn down a dog I believe is dangerous or a cat who is so difficult to medicate that I doubt we can care for it. But that is uncommon."

Daniela's current client pets include dogs, cats, fish, a turtle, and Elvis the pig. "He is a potbelly pig, but he is huge and very territorial. He bumps me to let me know I'm getting too close to his food. He has to wear suntan lotion, so I have to rub him down in the summer. He's very smart, but really big. We also used to care for an iguana, but that customer, who is still with us, had to give Mogley away."

Daniela emphasizes that taking care of pets means taking on a big responsibility, not only to the pet, but also to the client and to the client's home and furnishings. "We have insurance in case something happens, and our insurance has to match the homes we have keys to. For example, if an animal were injured while I was driving it somewhere, my insurance covers that. But I'd refuse to take a customer whose home had so many expensive things in it that my insurance wouldn't be enough to cover the expense if something was damaged in the home."

The people Daniela hires have to be self-motivated, responsible, and trustworthy. "It is a hard job to monitor, so I've hired close friends and people I know pretty well. We

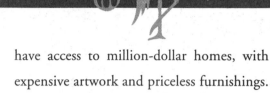

have access to million-dollar homes, with expensive artwork and priceless furnishings. To many of our clients, the most priceless of all is their animal. As we grow, I realize I will have to hire people I don't know well. That will be hard."

Do not let anyone discourage you from this business. This work is something to be proud of. People are grateful and appreciate the service.

No Dog for Daniela

Daniela grew up in Alexandria, VA, where she still lives. "I used to beg my mom to get a dog, but she refused. We had a cat, Pee Wee, and a bird, Tweety. I told her when I grew up I was going to have a house full of dogs, but she said by then I'd change my mind." Daniela laughs. "Now she's eating her words."

Daniela wanted to be a vet, but was not focused in school, so she didn't have what was needed to get into vet school. She took her talent and interest for fashion and attended the Fashion Institute of Technology in New York City. When she graduated, she came back to Alexandria and got a job with Nordstrom department store, which was just opening.

Working there 8 years was a great foundation for her business, Daniela says. She progressed to assistant manager, then manager of women's active sports, then merchandise manager's assistant to the men's division. "I got motivated and developed skills that I believe have helped me.

"The bottom line is keeping the customer.

CAREER CHECKLIST ✓

This career is for you if you ...

- Like people and understand good customer service

- Have high energy and can pace yourself

- Want to spend your time, even weekends, doing this

- Genuinely love animals

- Are trustworthy and responsible

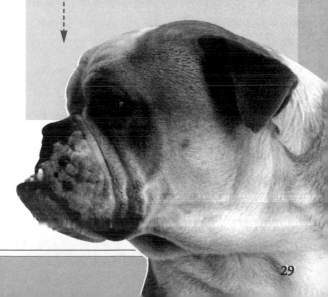

GROUNDBREAKERS

Rachel Carson, born 1907, was a zoologist. Her concern for the damage that pesticides and other poisonous chemicals caused to plants and animals led her to write Silent Spring *in 1962. This groundbreaking work raised awareness and was the start of the movement to save the environment.*

The Rachel Carson Council, Inc., has information about her life and her work (another book she wrote is Edge of the Sea). *Ask the Council about the Junior Scholar program. Contact them at 8940 Jones Mill Road, Chevy Chase, MD 20815, (301) 652-1877.*

We're providing a service. We do what customers want us to do, because the customer is the boss. We even have people who set up play dates for their pets and birthday parties."

Daniela met Steve through friends. When they married, both held jobs (retail and restaurant) where they worked long days, weekends, and holidays. Then they decided to buy a business. "We bought the business before Jackie was born," says Daniela. "I wanted to do something that would let me be close to my daughter and let me spend more time with her." By the time her daughter was 2, the business was bringing in enough money to equal Daniela's retail salary, and she left her job at Nordstrom. Steve still works a few days a month at the restaurant as a wine consultant.

The Dog Spa Dream

The next step for Privileged Pets may be a new venture—a spa for dogs. Many customers want Daniela to board their pets, but she doesn't offer that service. The spa would be just for dogs and offer a

It is a very successful way to make a living. Our charges start at $10 for a half hour visit/walk and go up depending on what else we do.

"vacation" for the dog when the owners go on vacation—special meals, social activities, chiropractic care, massages, baths, and deluxe sleeping area. "So many people don't want to leave their pets in a kennel or home alone. There are a few spas around the country that do well, but none in our area, so we are thinking about it."

Then, too, Steve wants to own his own restaurant some day. Maybe a spa and restaurant? Maybe later.

Jane Seigler

OWNER AND OPERATOR, **Reddemeade Equestrian Center,**
Silver Spring, MD

Major in International Relations. Law Degree

Horse Farm
owner

In Jeans and Horse Crazy

"There is a horse-crazy gene and it's not inherited," says Jane Seigler, who runs a riding stable and horse farm. "So many parents who have no interest in horses say that from the time their child could talk, it's been nothing but horses."

Jane knows she has the gene. She thinks it is fun to run a 7-days-a-week, year-round riding stable and horse farm. One of the largest facilities of its kind in Maryland, Reddemeade has 64 horses and a staff of 25. Jane, her husband, Paul, and another person own the property, but Jane is the main operator of the business. Her small office, in the center of a stable barn, has a window that looks out on a large indoor arena where students take private lessons and classes on horsemanship are held. On her desk are advertising flyers and newsletters promoting the various programs at Reddemeade.

- *Owners pay themselves a salary, also get profits from business*
- *Entry-level worker, minimum wage*
- *Hired Stable manager $20,000 to $60,000*
- *Trainers $15,000 to $45,000*
- *Jockeys $5,000 to several million, average $15,000*

Source: Encyclopedia of Careers and Vocational Guidance

JANE'S CAREER PATH

Rides horses in leisure
time

Graduates
college

Marries
Paul

School Horses Treasured

"We offer three services," says Jane. "First, we teach riding lessons to students of all ages and levels. For this we use one third of our horses. They are 'school horses,' trained to teach riding, and worth their weight in gold. The first thing a student has to learn is to control her body while on a moving horse. The horse's job is to ignore 90 percent of what a rider says to the horse through her body movements (which is the way the rider communicates). These horses are kind, less sensitive, and so

To do well in the business, the trick is to love the horses, but you have to at least like the people. I strongly encourage educating yourself and having some type of employment experience outside the horse world.

Gets law degree,
Editor of Law
Review

Moves to Maryland

Passes DC
bar, works
as lawyer

tolerant of unintended bouncing and jostling as the beginner learns body control. When we find horses with this type of temperament, we train them to be school horses."

The second service is called Equishare. Reddemeade provides quality riding horses to experienced riders who don't own their own horses. Jane believes this program, developed in 1986, may be the only one in the United States. Membership fees in the Equishare program can buy unlimited riding or riding 2 days per week, and there are other benefits.

"This is a special market niche," says Jane. "We have mostly adult, working people who have a good amount of riding experience. They may be in this area temporarily and have left a horse behind. There are also people who rode as youngsters and got away from it. Now they are working, and don't have time to own a horse, which is a large

time commitment, but they enjoy spending their leisure time riding."

Equishare also appeals to people who have taken many lessons, have learned to ride, and want to ride a more responsive horse, but are not ready for ownership. The Equishare horses are responsive and better trained than many privately owned horses because they are ridden frequently and continuously trained by professionals.

Jane's third service is boarding—providing a stall, feeding, and care/exercise for privately owned horses.

JANE'S CAREER PATH

Starts riding stable,
works part-time

Becomes full-time
owner/operator

Life Is Never Boring

"The fact that there is no typical day is one of the fun things about this job," says Jane. "But I try at some point each day to ride my own two horses. They need to be exercised and trained every day."

Jane competes in horse shows in what is called dressage, a French word that means training. "One of the nice things about the dressage competition is the judges give you feedback about how you and your horse are doing in the series of movements that show how well you've trained your horse," says Jane. She is always taking lessons and clinics and has read extensively to educate herself, a never-ending process.

Some days, Jane has to ride and train customers' horses. Several days she teaches, mostly private lessons, and one group lesson. Sometimes she cares for a sick animal or arranges its trip to a vet.

The rest of the time she runs the business—marketing/advertising to bring in new customers, handling paperwork, and planning programs and activities—competitions, social events, seminars, and clinics. Horsemanship is more than learning to ride a horse, it's learning about horses and their care, so Reddemeade runs a lot of educational programs on various topics. At the 2-week, summer day-camp sessions, campers ride twice a day, but the rest of the time they learn about horse breeds, horse instincts, and what will keep horses healthy. They also learn about all the horse show competitions like dressage, hunter/jumper, show jumping, and the Olympics.

"Equestrian sports are among the very few sports that are gender blind, there are no barriers for women to overcome. There are no divisions. In the Olympics, men and women compete head to head."

A Hard-Working Staff

An important part of Jane's success is knowing what her customers want and working with her staff to be sure the horses and the customers are well cared for. The work is hard. There is outside work in all kinds of weather, and there won't come back if the staff is too critical, or isn't friendly and helpful."

Reddemeade's 25 staff members work part-time or full-time. There are 15 instructors giving lessons on varied schedules. For the other 10, the day is structured around caring for the horses. "Horses are designed to be continuous grazers, but do well being fed in the morning and evening. Then we give a

You will need people skills and business skills, because most of your customers and clients are people from outside the horse world who expect you to be a professional business person.

must be the right balance between workload and pay to keep workers' morale high. "This is a service business, and our customers come to enjoy themselves. They

third feed of hay at night. At midday, we clean stalls. If an animal gets sick, we are here as long as it takes."

Jane always loved to ride, but never owned a horse until well out of school. She rode a fair amount in high school and a little bit in college, where she studied International Relations. She wanted to be a diplomat. She met her future husband, Paul, at college. "When he proposed, I told him I would only marry him on the condition that we would have horses. He agreed. He has come to love horses as much as I do."

After graduation, the couple moved to Princeton where Paul got his graduate degree

Good horsemanship takes brains and brawn. No one can out muscle a horse. You need tact, intelligence, and sensitivity as well as strength to win a horse's cooperation and trust. Put time in to figure out your horse and work out a way to communicate.

and Jane did administrative work for a software company while she decided what she wanted to do with her life. She decided on law and attended Rutgers Law School, where she earned such honors as editor in chief of the *Rutgers Law Review*.

When Jane and Paul moved to work in the Washington, DC, area, they settled in the Maryland countryside so they could have horses. Jane got back into riding and did part-time teaching while working full-time as a lawyer. Then they bought property and started building the business. For about 9 years Jane worked full-time and supervised the business as it grew. In 1993 she was ready to devote full-time to the horse farm.

"This is a great industry for women because parts of it are so beautiful and elegant, and parts allow you to do any amount of physical or mechanical work you want. There are no barriers."

CAREER CHECKLIST ✓

This career is for you if you ...

- Are willing to do hard physical work outdoors
- Can handle heartaches of sick or injured horses
- Will be open-minded and keep learning
- Love horses but also like people

Megan Dudek

RAPTOR HANDLER/INTERPRETER, **The Baltimore Zoo, MD**

Major in Anthropology

Bird Handler/
Interpreter

Miss Meg the Zookeeper

"Miss Meg the zoo lady" wears a heavy glove that covers her left arm up to the elbow. On it sits Storm, a Red Shouldered Hawk, who pulls at her shirt. She explains to the children watching that Storm is preening her, a sign of affection. "Storm was taken out of the wild as a chick by a young boy who hand-raised her. She is totally imprinted. That means she only identifies with humans and wasn't raised by a hawk. So she can't be released to the wild. Here is an animal that retains her wildness. She is still capable of hurting you, and she's not afraid of you. That's a bad combination."

Meg is in charge of the raptors, birds of prey, but she shows any of the animals at the Baltimore Zoo lab, which houses all animals featured in the zoo's educational programs. Most of the shows are performed at the zoo .

- Zookeepers and zoo technicians $17,000 to $35,000;
- Entry level, minimum wage

Source: Encyclopedia of Careers and Vocational Guidance

The local TV show Kindertime, where Meg is the zoo lady, is filmed at the zoo for later broadcast.

"I never thought I'd like that sort of thing, but it's fun. I think I was chosen because of my experience. My job is very much out in the public. When you work with animals in front of the public, you have to speak well, be sort of goofy, and be quick to ad lib."

The current rage in bird performances is free flight. When Meg returned from Minnesota, after a special training session with bird expert Steve Martin (who is her idol and mentor), she trained Storm to fly on command.

From Chopped Mice to Anklets

Meg does everything for the raptors, everything. She prepares their food which must be warm and sometimes chopped up—mice, chicks, quail, BOP (bird of prey food for zoo birds), and vitamins. Before feeding each bird is weighed. This determines how much food, weighed to the gram, the birds get to stay healthy. "If Storm weighs 5 grams over 2 pounds, she won't be motivated to fly." Cages must be cleaned every day and fresh water available for drinking and bathing.

These large birds require all kinds of equipment, and Meg must arrange to buy it

Graduates college,
▼ moves to St. Louis

Gets
▼ married

Raises endangered
▼ Guam Kingfisher at
St. Louis Zoo

or make it. For example, each bird has leather anklets, with swivels, and straps called jesses, so the handler can restrain it. The anklets must be made of kangaroo leather, and there is only one distributor in the United States who can legally sell the leather. "The equipment must be customized for each bird. That's why the sport of falconry can be expensive. This part of my job is very involved, detail oriented, and time consuming."

"In order for the birds to trust you, you have to build and maintain a positive relationship. I handle them, have training sessions, play ball, just 'hang out' with the birds," says Meg. She also helps out other departments with training and participates in special events and celebrations at the zoo.

Primates Changed Meg's Life

There was never a question—Meg would work in a zoo someday. Her uncle was a zookeeper at the Lincoln Park Zoo in Chicago, and he often took Meg there as a child. When she was about 17, she and 200 others applied for 10 summer internships at the Brookfield Zoo in the Chicago area.

"I was the youngest, but I think I got it because I was so motivated, so excited, and so willing to do anything. I always thought I wanted to be a dolphin trainer, but there was a spot in the primates area. I just fell in love. It changed my whole career path—in college I studied anthropology instead of biology. It was so wonderful. I worked with the keepers, they let me do everything that they did and included me when they cared for large apes."

The next summer, Meg was hired for the

children's zoo to do animal shows and be a keeper. "I loved it. I had a miniature pig named Maya (who only understood Spanish, and played basketball) and a Capuchan monkey who did horrible things to me in front of the public. She'd been trained with punishment in a program for the

thought it was so funny. It was a good lesson to people, and they changed their minds about wanting a pet monkey. There was a narrator for the shows and we also had goats, and llamas." Meg worked there three summers during her college years, and she discovered she liked all the animals.

Animals can sense fear, so you learn early not to be afraid.

disabled at a university, but didn't work out. She maintained some of the behaviors, like putting a straw in a drink, but then she'd do whacko things like shove it in my face, jump on my head, pull my hair. People loved it; they

While home on a holiday break, Meg met her future husband, Steve, at a New Year's Eve party. When she graduated from Northern Illinois University in DeKalb, she moved to join him in St. Louis, MO, where he was attending medical school.

While trying to get a job at the St. Louis

zoo, Meg worked at a coffee store at a mall. "At Christmas time I was talking with a customer, explaining what I really wanted to do, and she said, 'I know the President of the Board over there and I'm going to give him a call.' Sure enough, the next day he called and asked for my resume. So I started part-time at the children's zoo there. After about 9 months, a full-time position opened in the bird department. That's when I got my love for birds."

A Gift of Understanding

Even though Meg had no actual experience with birds, she says what the zoo wanted was a keeper, a person who knows how to "read" animals.

"Your ability to read an animal, to interact with an animal, you're born with it. I've trained keepers, but some people just don't have it. I can't train someone to look at a bird and really know what is going on in that bird's head. When you apply for a job there is a test—they show you an animal and ask what's going on here? I've always been able to sense what is going on. I think most keepers find their way to this job because of that gift.

"It's hard to explain, but I can recognize it.

CAREER CHECKLIST ✓

This career is for you if you ...

Understand animal behavior and are sensitive to their feelings

Are physically fit

Love animals and teaching about animals

Don't mind working weekends and holidays

GROUNDBREAKERS

Dian Fossey, previously an occupational therapist, went to Africa in 1966 where, through observation, she came to know and understand the mountain gorillas. She became their champion against poachers. She was brutally murdered in December 1985.

Two biographies are Woman in the Mists *by Farley Mowat. (1987). New York: Warner Books; and* The Dark Romance of Dian Fossey *by Harold T. P. Hayes. (1990). New York: Simon & Schuster.*

You have to be good at picking up subtle cues. Birds actually mask problems, so by the time a bird looks sick, it's too late. You have to notice it way before, by the way it shifts its eyes, or the pupils dilate, or feathers are out of place. I can also feel tension through my glove and can tell if I need to put the bird back on its perch. My really true love is being a keeper."

At first Meg moved around, filling in on others' days off, working where she was needed. Later she worked full-time in the bird house's artificial-incubation and hand rearing area for endangered birds. "I was in charge of incubating eggs from crane chicks, vultures, penguins, Bateleur eagles—all kinds, plus care of breeding pairs in cages. I would bring birds home, because you had to feed the babies every few hours. My husband thought it was really neat, bringing eagle chicks home, but he wasn't too thrilled at keeping ground rat in our refrigerator."

Saving a Rare Bird

The zoo had a pair of Guam Kingfishers, (now extinct on Guam and only about 60 pairs in captivity in the world). "No one expected it, but one day I found their egg. I carefully removed it and placed it in the incubator. I turned it 5, 6 times a day and it hatched. She grew up and hated me, which means I raised her right. At age 25 I had raised a Guam Kingfisher. I contributed to the survival of the species. It was a wonderful feeling."

Meg wanted to get large carnivore experience. "It's sort of the highest level you can get as a keeper and comes after years of experience. A sea lion trainer position opened, to do shows, and I got that job. I liked the animals, but it wasn't what I thought it would be. I was working with a man who had 25 years of experience and who didn't appreciate a young woman coming in to work with him (25 years ago there were few women in the business). It became too difficult, so after a year I moved into the carnivore unit as a keeper. I worked mostly with the bears—grizzlies, polar bears, black bears—and cheetahs. There were 7 men keepers and 2 of us women. When the other keeper went in with the cheetahs, I went with her and we played with the cheetahs. When my friends asked if I'd been afraid, I realized it hadn't occurred to me to be afraid. That was when I knew that I was exactly in the place I needed to be, doing what I needed to be doing."

"I've been injured and attacked, but have never been afraid. Animals can sense fear, so you learn early not to be afraid. The cheetahs purr, push you down and get on top of you, even lick you, and their tongue really hurts, but I loved it."

When Meg's husband got his residency, the couple moved to Baltimore. Meg got a job at the Baltimore Zoo working with giraffes. The zoo's director knew Meg because he had just left the position of assistant director of the St. Louis Zoo. Two years ago, when the bird show position of raptor handler/interpreter came open, Meg took it.

"I love going to work and miss the birds on my days off. It is common for zoo keepers not to have kids. The animals are their kids. But I think you can have a family and enjoy your job too. It's a hard decision to make." Meg is expecting a child in early summer and plans to work part-time.

Laura Thompson-Olais

ECOLOGIST, HEAD OF INTERNATIONAL GROUP ON PRONGHORNS,
Cabeza Prieta Refuge, AZ

Major in Wildlife Management

Wildlife Management

Bears and Pigs and Pronghorn—Oh My

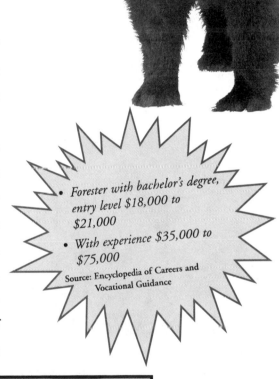

Laura Thompson-Olais grew up in New York City and lived in a big apartment building with no yard to play in. But she always knew she wanted to work outdoors. Now she's a wildlife ecologist, a person who studies plants and animals and tries to understand how they can thrive in a particular environment, such as the desert. Laura has worked with wild pigs, black bears, abandoned pet burros that became wild, bald eagles, and pronghorn, an animal related to the antelope. Laura is also the wife of Cheto Olais and the mother of 3-year-old Eliana and 1-year-old Kelek.

Laura works 30 hours a week at Cabeza Prieta Wildlife Refuge in Southwestern Arizona. Cabeza Prieta means black head in Spanish. The Refuge is 860,000 acres of national wildlife refuge, 93 percent of which is wilderness, in one of the

- *Forester with bachelor's degree, entry level $18,000 to $21,000*
- *With experience $35,000 to $75,000*

Source: Encyclopedia of Careers and Vocational Guidance

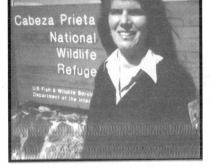

most interesting deserts on earth. There are more than 1,000 species of plants in the area and several endangered animal species. One endangered subspecies, the Sonoran prong-

Tohono O'odham, whose people live and work on an Indian reservation next to the refuge; (3) the Mexican government, which shares a 56-mile border with the refuge; (4)

House cleaning was a good job because I could set my own hours and my own pay.

horn, is only found in the Southwestern United States and Mexico. It feeds on desert cactus and exists where other pronghorn cannot.

But the number of pronghorn is decreasing. Laura is the head of a working group that includes five groups—representatives from (1) the Refuge; (2) the Indian nation of

the Air Force, whose Barry Goldwater air-testing range overlays Cabeza Prieta Refuge land; and (5) the state of Arizona. Together these groups must decide on a policy that will help the pronghorn to survive and increase in number.

Laura started college at New Rochelle College in Iona, NY. After 2 years, she knew

she wanted to study wildlife management. She chose California and enrolled in Humboldt State University near the Oregon border and in the middle of the Redwood Forest, because it had a good wildlife management program. "I knew I didn't want to go to vet school or to just major in biology or zoology."

Laura paid for most of the cost of college herself. To earn money during college, she helped a botanist type a book he had written, she worked at the California State Park Service in the visitors center one summer, and she

cleaned houses. "House cleaning was actually a good job," she says, "because I could set my own hours and my own pay."

Jill of All Trades

Through the school's cooperative education program, Laura got a job with the National Park Service. She worked at Pinnacles National Monument near San Jose, CA, doing pretty much everything that needed to be done—inter-

51

LAURA'S CAREER PATH

Heads pronghorn
project at Cabeza
Prieta Refuge

Decides to work
part-time

pretation in the visitors' center, trail maintenance, firefighting, and search and rescue work. She worked with visitors, presenting natural history discussions, campfire programs, and nature walks. She studied wild pigs to see how many were living

I got about 17 volunteers to patrol the campgrounds to see that people had their food properly stored away so bears couldn't get it. We put radio collars on the bears so we could track them.

in the area and what their feeding habits were.

Her next job with the National Park Service was at Joshua Tree National Monument in Southern California, which is in the Mojave desert. Here one of her jobs was to help capture and get wild burros out of the monument as they were not native to the area.

Then Laura got a job at Sequoia King Canyon National Park near Fresno, CA, as a biological technician. She spent most of her time teaching people about the black bears in the park. "People would come into the park with their food, and the black bears would break into their cars or come into camp and try to get food. Unfortunately, if a bear became a nuisance it would have to be killed. I thought that was very wrong, because it wasn't the bear's fault. It was the people's fault. So I got about 17 volunteers to patrol the campgrounds to see that people had their food properly stored away so bears couldn't get it. We put radio collars on the bears so we could track them." This meant that she and the volunteers had to capture the bears and use a tranquilizer gun to immobilize them.

Laura spent lots of time going to elementary schools and talking to kids about the

Attitude is everything. If you have a good attitude, you can roll with the punches.

habits of black bears and what to do if you camp in the park. "That was great because kids are such a receptive audience," Laura says. "They would go home and teach their parents."

At Pinnacles, Laura had met her future husband, who works for the National Park Service in law enforcement. When he got a job at Lava Beds National Monument in Northern California, Laura found a job with the National Forest Service at Modoc National Forest working with the Air Force as a wildlife biologist. There she worked on counting spotted owls, vernal pools that are caused by seasonal rains, and studying bald eagles. Sometimes she had to tell a government agency that employees had done something that was against environmental laws and help them figure out how they could fix

their mistake. That's how Laura learned to work with more than one government agency at the same time.

Time for Family Important

Laura got married in 1991. Not too long after that, her husband got a job at the Organ Pipe Monument in Arizona. So Laura looked for a job in Arizona. Her experience working with the Air Force helped her get the job at Cabeza Prieta. She lives at Organ Pipe Cactus Monument, which is in the Sonoran desert and is 40 miles from her work. Each workday she takes her daughter and son through the desert to Ajo, a town of 3,000 people, where the Refuge headquarters is, to a baby-sitter. "When we get home, I spend time with my kids. That's an important part of my life right now," Laura says. "After all, children are the future of our country."

Until recently Laura was the Acting Refuge Manager for Cabeza Prieta, one of the biggest wilderness refuges in the lower 48 states, a job she got when her boss had to quit because of poor health. She decided not to apply for the position of Refuge Manager so that she could spend more time with her family, because the job of running a wildlife refuge is a demanding one. As acting director, Laura had to supervise a staff of employees and volunteers and attend many meetings. Sometimes she had as many as four meetings a week.

"You have to have good supervisory skills, know how to mediate between different points of view, know how to negotiate well, and know how and when to use psychology to get the job done. A former boss in the park service told me to always keep things in perspective. That advice has been really valuable. Sometimes people won't agree with you. You have to keep your sight on the goal you want to accomplish."

Laura enjoys her work at the Refuge as head of the pronghorn project. Right now 30 hours a week seems right, as she devotes that extra nonwork time to her family.

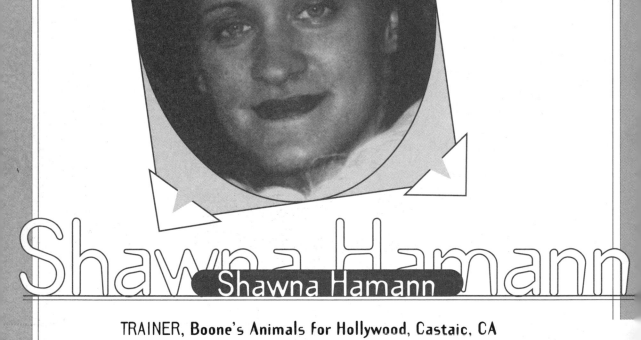

Shawna Hamann

Shawna Hamann

TRAINER, Boone's Animals for Hollywood, Castaic, CA

Graduate, Moorpark College Teaching Zoo

Exotic Animal
Trainer

Acting Coach to the Stars

Watching mice scamper across the screen in the movie "Mouse Hunt" was a kick for Shawna Hamann. She was busy trying to identify each "actor."

"I kept saying 'that's so and so' and 'so and so did that.' My boyfriend had to tell me to be quiet," Shawna says.

Shawna knew which mouse was which because she helped train them for the movie. A full-time animal trainer, who has worked for Boone's Animals for Hollywood for about 3 years, Shawna works with everything from camels to chimpanzees to, of course, mice.

She trains animals for movies, television shows, and commercials. Movie work requires long hours—14- to 16-hour days— but gives Shawna a chance to travel to the locations where the shows are being made. So far Shawna, who is 21, has been to Texas and New York and has done a lot of filming in the California desert.

Shawna is a member of the union Teamsters Local 339, and she earns $30 an hour

Among other things, her work has taught her that mice are smart and that camels get a bad rap. "Everyone seems to think camels spit, but I haven't seen them."

You have to make the animal believe it can't hurt you.

Mice Are Fun

While working on Mouse Hunt, which was released December 1997, Shawna found the mice "were more fun than we thought they would be. They really learned a lot. They had to learn to run from one point to another. They were taught to go to a 'mark,' like actors—they had to put their feet on a mark for the camera.

"They were taught to go to the bed and climb under the covers. They could turn on a radio. They ran through a maze in the kitchen. There was a lot of climbing and jumping." Praise and food are an animal train-er's tools. "With mice, a lot of it was food." In all cases, the American Humane Association makes sure the animals are well treated.

Now, Shawna is working full-time on the television series "7th Heaven" where she trains Happy, a 2-year-old terrier mix, who was "discovered" at a local animal shelter.

"Happy is Simon's dog (actor David Gallagher is Simon). She's always following him around the house," according to

Studies
▼ exotic
animal training

Get job
▼ with Boone's

Trains Happy
▼ for TV

Shawna. Happy spends most of her "off duty" time with the young actors on the show or sometimes playing with Shawna's own puppies. (Shawna has a dog and a puppy that are her personal pets.)

"Happy has her own trailer, her own bathroom. She's treated well. She's usually on the set three or four days a week," Shawna says. Because the law limits how many hours "7th Heaven's" child actors can work, Shawna usually has an 8-hour day. But "that's not typical of the animal business."

Since Happy is supposed to be a family dog, "she doesn't do a lot of tricks. She can cover her eyes or she will sit up and beg. She gives kisses. Mostly she's on the bed, hanging out with the kids, or sitting next to them at the dinner table," Shawna says.

"We did one episode where one of older kids brought home a marijuana joint and Happy had to pick it up and bring it to their dad."

It takes lots of patience to teach Happy

tricks like picking things up and dropping them on command. And it takes lots of praise and rewards of her favorite foods—chicken and hot dogs. Shawna insists that "Happy is more into praise than food."

Lucky to Live Near Training

Shawna was only 6 or 7 when she decided she wanted to be an animal trainer. Growing up in Southern California "we had tons of animals—cats and dogs and rabbits and birds. Pretty much everything that was legal. We always had a house full."

Shawna didn't try to train pets when she was young, but "I was always interested. At a movie, I'd always wait till the end to see who the animal trainer was."

That's probably because growing up in Castaic, Calif., Shawna lived about 10 min-

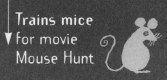
Being really strong isn't all that much of an advantage. Some animals could overpower anybody.

utes from Moorpark College, a community college that has an exotic animal training program.

"When I was in school, we went on a field trip there. I was pretty lucky to live so close by," Shawna says. As soon as she finished high school, Shawna knew where to go to follow her dream of becoming an animal trainer. She enrolled in Moorpark's Exotic Animal Training and Management Program.

The exotic animal program is the only one of its kind, according to Mara Rodriguez, education and entertainment coordinator at Moorpark College. The 22-month-long pro-

gram attracts students from all over the world. Students from California pay regular community college fees while out-of-state students pay extra fees. The program combines classroom study in subjects such as anatomy and animal behavior with intense, hands-on training of exotic animals.

At the school, students arrive at 6 every morning to do the cleaning and feeding chores. It's a lot of fun, but it's a lot of hard work. For a lot of people, waking up and coming in before the sun is up is the hardest part.

"It was pretty hard," Shawna remembers.

Students usually take about 21 units of college courses a semester. At the same time, they had to clean out the animal cages. "We would take turns once a week spending the night to make sure the animals were okay. I would start cleaning at 6 a.m. and go to classes at around 8. I wouldn't get home until around 6 at night."

No Business Like Show Business

While she was in school, Shawna found she especially liked doing shows in front of people and realized she most wanted to train animals for the movies. As part of the Moorpark program, the instructor and student take animals to schools, hospitals, camps, and churches for educational shows. Twenty animals including foxes, monkeys, reptiles, and owls—are part of the touring educational program. In addition, the school has mountain lions, water buffalo, camels, tigers, and sea lions.

Girls love sea lions and animal training in general, according to Shawna. In her class of 50 there were 44 girls and about 6 guys. This is a woman-dominated program and field

and has been for the past 15 years, perhaps because it's not seen as a high-profile, high-paying kind of job. With all the women in the profession, Shawna hasn't found discrimination on the job.

While it may not be seen as a high-paying job, you can earn a living being an animal trainer. Some animal parks pay only minimum wage, but many public zoos pay about $20 an hour. Shawna is a member of the union Teamsters Local 339, and she earns $30 an hour. She just bought her own house with a huge yard in Castaic where she grew up, just north of Los Angeles.

Shawna recommends that any girl who is thinking about a career as an animal trainer get experience working with animals. It can be pet sitting or working at a clinic or local animal shelter. She did volunteer work at a veterinarian's clinic during high school. "I

GROUNDBREAKERS

Joy Adamson grew up in Austria, but spent more than 30 years in Kenya.
Her husband was a game warden.
She painted and wrote—her best known books about raising lion cubs are Born Free, Living Free, *and* Forever Free.
Until her death, she traveled and spoke to many audiences about helping endangered species.
Her autobiography is titled The Searching Spirit (1978).

worked at a ranch for a little while where friends of mine had domestic animals and horses."

"There are probably about 400 people who apply to Moorpark and they only take 50 a year" in the exotic animal program, Shawna says. "The more volunteering you do, the better your chances. In addition you find out if that's what you want to do. It has to be something you want to do or it's not worth all the work."

Shawna advises girls to get letters of recommendation from places where they are known, like the veterinary office where they take their pets or places where they volunteer.

It's a good idea to be basically physically fit if you want to be a trainer, says Shawna, who studied gymnastics when she was young. But being really strong isn't all that much of an advantage. Some animals could overpower anybody, there's no way to be as strong as they are. For example, chimpanzees are seven times stronger than the average human male and could throw you across the room.

Shawna says you have to show you are confident. "You have to have good self-esteem and a positive image when you walk into the cage. You have to make the animal believe it can't hurt you."

It may sound funny, but taking classes in public speaking can help if you want to be an animal trainer. That's because trainers often do shows and present animals to the public. A lot of people assume if you're working with animals you don't need much personality—that's wrong. To be the best in this field, it's good attitude and good personality that gets you work.

"A lot of people think you don't have to like people, just be able to work with animals. But in production companies you have to be able to work with people. I do interviews sometimes for the series, and I have to be comfortable" with public speaking.

With all her work, Shawna doesn't have much leisure time for hobbies, but she's not complaining. "I love what I do. I've always known this is what I want to do," she says. "I love to get outside and not be cooped up."

Another of the things Shawna really likes about her job is the variety. "I'll always be learning something—even if I'm in this business for 25 years."

CAREER CHECKLIST

This career is for you if you ...

Are not afraid of wild animals

Have the stamina to work many hours, long days

Love training animals

Are able to speak to groups of people

Like to travel

Lydia Wade

Lydia Wade

TRAINER, OWNER, **Blue Ridge Assistance Dogs, Manassas, VA**

Assistance
Dog Trainer

From Sweet Pup to Trusted Companion

Sit, stay, down, heel—learning these commands is just the beginning of a long process for a dog selected to become a service dog or a social/therapy dog. Lydia Wade's business provides these types of assistance dogs to individuals with disabilities. Service dogs help people who need assistance with mobility or balance. They may be in a wheel chair, can't move around well, and have limited movement. The dogs learn to pick up dropped or needed items, turn lights on and off, pull a wheelchair, open doors, and push elevator buttons. Social/therapy dogs help people by offering unconditional love, acceptance, and social companionship. They can also help with speech, and with physical and psychological therapies.

Lydia selects, raises, trains, and places the dogs. She chooses the puppies and dogs from shelters, and from breeders who specialize in

- Business owner pays self salary and gets business profit
- Hired trainers entry level, minimum wage
- With experience $25,000 to $50,000

Source: Encyclopedia of Careers and Vocational Guidance

LYDIA'S CAREER PATH

Reads book about seeing eye dogs

Studies landscape architecture

Gets married

assistance dogs. "I look in their eyes for a sweet look, dogs that love everyone. But of those selected, only 25 percent make it. As you get to know them you might find something that will disqualify them—they don't like people in brown hats or they can be distracted and will chase things."

After selection, the dogs move into Lydia's kennel/house and Lydia raises them. They need constant attention. The emphasis is on giving and receiving love. Lydia believes in positive reinforcement and motivation, not punishment, as she teaches basic behavior commands. "I use choke chains with a stopper on them, not shock collars. The dog has to respond and be corrected by voice. Most people won't have the strength or ability to control the dog by physical movement."

When the dog is a little over a year, the assistance training begins at "college," advanced skill training. Now the dog learns to open doors, pick up items, not only pull the wheelchair but set its brakes, even get things out of the refrigerator. The dog learns to place its elbows in the person's lap. In that way it can deliver items picked up and get hugged and petted. The commands to perform all these "tricks" are as short as possible, so they will be easy for persons with disabilities to pronounce. When the dog is mature enough to have good house manners and know that it has a job to do, the person with a disability is trained with the dog and they become a team.

66

Constant Commitment

"The relationship is different than with a pet, it's an even deeper relationship," says Lydia. "You are with the dog 24 hours. When you are home and when you go out in public, the dog has a job to help you." (Whenever an assistance dog is in public and has a vest, cap, backpack, or harness on, it is working and should never be interrupted, disturbed, or distracted without permission from the owner. Lydia's Blue Ridge dogs wear her company's colors. Their backpacks are purple with turquoise trim).

"The dogs have to obey the commands in lots of different places. They learn to sit and

You have to be open to different ideas. No one way is right, what works on one dog may not work with another.

lie down on carpet, on concrete, in grass, on linoleum—when it is quiet or noisy. The variety keeps them from getting bored with repetitions of the same command. We go to the mall, grocery stores, libraries, parades, big events with lots of people. We ride trains, subways, and go on airplanes. The laws are different in every state. In Virginia, trainers have the same rights as the person with disabilities. So I take the dogs to restaurants and other places where dogs are not normally welcomed."

The dogs are usually mature enough to be placed with a person when they are between a year and one-half and two years of age, depending on each individual dog's maturity and skill level. During this time, Lydia evaluates the dogs' personalities, their energy levels, and how they learn. She uses this information to help her match the individual with disabilities with the right dog. "It is like a marriage. If you are a quiet person, like to stay around the house and not always be on the go or out with lots of people, you want a less energetic dog, one who will be happy to lie down near you and not whine about being still."

When the dog is trained, Lydia teaches the applicant how to work with the dog so they are a team. "The person needs to learn to control the dog. I teach how the dog thinks and learns. Because at the most you have the dog's attention for 3 seconds, you have to be quick. It takes about 2 weeks of intensive work, which is very fatiguing on the person. But it's fun to see the bond of love grow between them and see the person begin to feel more independent." Throughout the team's life together, Lydia offers follow-up visits and help to be sure the communication between the person and dog is working.

As owner of the business, Lydia has to keep records of expenses, make sure that the animals' medical records are up to date, handle the application process, and know the laws with respect to assistance dogs. She keeps in touch with other trainers and attends conferences to keep up to date with trends in the field.

She also must ask people for money. Lydia's charges can run from $10,000 to $25,000 for a trained dog. The individuals themselves are charged on a sliding scale according to ability to pay. Donations make up the difference. Often the individual with disability can't afford to pay, so generous people and organizations donate money, which Lydia puts into a general "scholarship fund" or a special fund in the individual's name. (In the state of Montana, Medicaid will make payment for the dog, its care, and its food in some cases. Activitists are working to get other states to do the same.)

CAREER CHECKLIST

This career is for you if you ...

Have a love for dogs and fascination of how they learn

Understand personality traits and how to match people with dogs

Are patient

Are somewhat comfortable working with people with disabilities

Are not afraid to ask for donations

GROUNDBREAKERS

Barbara Woodhouse was born in

Dublin in 1910.

Over the course of 30 years,

she personally trained 17,000 dogs

and their owners in her

weekend courses.

She taught perfect obedience to

basic commands in 6 and

a half hours.

She has appeared on TV's "60

Minutes," and her books and TV

program "Training Dogs the

Woodhouse Way"

(British Broadcasting Company) were

enormously popular in the

United States.

A Search for Training

When Lydia decided she wanted to be a trainer, she contacted many people before she found someone who offered assistance-dog training. The founder of Canine Companions for Independence, Dr. Bonita Bergin, had started a new organization for eduction, research, and development, The Assistance Dog Institute. She offered a 6-weeks training session. The tuition was $2,500, and the trainees had to pay for their hotel, food, and transportation (about $2,500).

"It was very intensive. The first 2 weeks we actually had to sit in wheelchairs and work with different dogs. We could get out of the chair only in our room at night. This gave us insight into what the person with limited mobility experienced. The next 2 weeks we trained dogs—some were fully trained and some were just learning. The last 2 weeks we interviewed disabled people who wanted dogs, and we placed dogs. Some dogs made it, some didn't. We worked with all different kinds of disabilities, both physical and mental. We learned from trial and error and from each other. Most important, we learned to listen to ourselves and our own instincts. At the end I knew 'I can do this.' "

Lydia enjoys her workplace. One large room provides kennel and training space and one smaller room serves as living/office/training area. There is a fenced exercise yard. The building is a former barn on the family property in the countryside near Manassas, VA. Lydia lives in an apartment in her mother's house, where she has her pet cats and pet dogs.

Inspired by a Book

When Lydia was in elementary school, she was fascinated by a book she read, *First Lady of the Seeing Eye*, a true story about dogs for the blind. Ever since Lydia can remember, her grandmother appreciated the mystery of animals and that they are a gift. All of her family showed caring and compassion for all animals. Lydia has had pets since she was born. She picked out her first puppy, a Siberian Husky, when she was two. It took a long time for Lydia to find a path that fit her interests. She knew she wanted to work outdoors, but she also wanted to work with people. She studied landscape architecture at college, but finally decided against that career. When she went to change her major after 3 years, she didn't have enough credits in the right courses and would have had to start over. So she left college and returned home to decide what to do. She worked for a couple of veterinarians in the area. She realized she wanted to educate people about animals and the helping relationships and bonds that they form with people.

"I married my best friend. But we were total opposites. I was raised nonviolent, he was raised with weapons all over the place. We were married 7 years, during which I did secretarial work and he did police work in different Virginia cities. I wasn't able to continue college or raise puppies because my husband didn't want me to." When the couple decided to divorce, Lydia moved to her mother's home in Manassas. "I realized divorce was for the best. Now I could do what I wanted to do—train dogs for disabled people."

Claudia Luke

CO-DIRECTOR, Sweeney Granite Mountains Desert Research Center, Mojave Desert, CA and Adjunct Professor, University of California, Riverside

Major in Zoology, Ph.D. Herpetology

Zoologist
Herpetologist

Luke's Lizards and Other Desert Creatures

Claudia Luke came home from her fifth-grade class one day and asked her mother, "What do you call a person who studies animals?" They looked it up in the dictionary and found zoologist.

Today Claudia is a zoologist and co-director of the Sweeney Granite Mountains Desert Research Center in California's Mojave Desert. She studies rare desert tortoises and other animals. Claudia is also a university professor. Her specialty is herpetology—the branch of zoology that studies reptiles and amphibians such as snakes, lizards, turtles, frogs, and salamanders.

When Claudia was a girl, her family liked to go backpacking. Claudia always wanted to learn about the mysterious lives of animals. "I thought if I just sat still enough, I could be part of the animals around me," she says.

Claudia's mother helped her find a course

- Starting pay $13.37 per hour, $27,800 per year; mid-range $34,000 to $64,000

  Source: Encyclopedia of Careers and Vocational Guidance

on how to identify birds. Her mother always believed in Claudia's dream to study animals. But getting her education wasn't always fun for Claudia. High school biology class turned out to be "boring, dry, and flat," says Claudia. So she decided to get some experience with people who were already studying animals. She studied one year in junior college and worked as a laboratory researcher. That's one job a zoologist or biologist might have, but Claudia didn't like lab work. She wanted to study animals in their natural environment.

Monkeys and Lizards

Then Claudia went to the University of California at Berkeley. She paid her own way to spend a month in Kenya, Africa, to study the black and white colobus monkey. Claudia loved it.

The next summer she went to western Texas to work with a professor who studies a special kind of lizard. Claudia found lizards and then shot crickets through a straw to feed them. The professor wanted to find out if those lizards that got extra food lived longer.

Another professor at Berkeley asked her to work with him as a graduate student and study herpetology. She spent six years in graduate school—the average time for students in her field—making her living by teaching

part time. Teaching made her nervous at first. But when she stopped worrying so much about what students thought of her, she got good at it.

To earn her doctorate (PhD) degree, sultant in the San Francisco area. Companies that wanted to develop land and needed to know about rare animals that lived there hired Claudia to look for these

I like the exposed honesty of the desert landscape.

Claudia decided to do research on lizards in the desert. She found the desert really is the place for her. "I like the extremes in temperature, the exposed honesty of the landscape. I like the feeling of being small, of being a part of something bigger."

After graduation, Claudia worked as a con-

protected animals and write reports. It paid well, but Claudia wasn't satisfied, because she would write a report and never hear about the project again.

After about four years, she and Jim Andre, who is her partner In

Once you get the answer to something, you've got it for the first time ever.

work and in life, got the chance to be co-directors of the Desert Research Center in the Mojave. The center is one of 32 reserves managed by the University of California Natural Reserve System. Claudia, Jim, and two other people live in the desert, where the wild, undisturbed natural habitat is protected for education and scientific study.

Protecting the Environment

Claudia loves every part of her job. "Everything I do—whether it is administrative, research, scheduling, or fundraising—all relates back to protecting the area for research and education." As a field station director, Claudia doesn't have a daily or weekly schedule; and her job changes as new research projects begin.

Here are some of the things she might do in a typical day, which begins about 8 in the morning.

First, Claudia checks her email and responds to it and "snail" mail. Then she may do some purchasing tasks, like ordering supplies of solar batteries or tags for tagging specimens. When individuals or groups use the center's facilities for classes or field research, they must pay fees. Claudia figures what the costs are and does the billing.

Claudia acts as the center's host or public relations person. When a research group or class arrives, she shows visitors around, sees that they get settled in, and helps them with any supplies they might need, like hammers and nails to build a "temporary observation post." She also gives tours and explains the facilities to visitors, who may want to do research or hold classes. She tells visitors about the current research projects, shows examples of rock art (paintings by native Americans), and explains the center's "solar passive" design and use of alternative energy.

Organization of Biological Field Stations in Sydney, Australia.

Claudia consults with various people during the course of the day. She may talk with the center's steward, who is in charge of maintenance, about the best, most cost-efficient way to do a repair project. She may read a government environmental impact statement and offer her opinions. She may look over a Park Service plan and write her comments on how the plan affects the desert environment and the center's current research projects.

Claudia may also contact volunteers and ask them to help out with an upcoming project such as preparing an scientific insect collection. Then, the weekend they come she may work right alongside them.

Claudia enforces the reserve's rules. For example, people are told to drive only on the roads. Sometimes, someone drives off the road, perhaps running over desert grass and shrub. Claudia says, "I have to write them a nasty letter, explaining that such action is not permitted and if they continue, they won't be allowed to return to the reserve. It's not my favorite task."

The center is remote and has rather rustic facilities, so no large meetings are held there. Claudia often has telephone "meetings" with National Park Service employees or people from a regional or state agency. Sometimes Claudia is asked to be a speaker (for example, she spoke at University of California, Riverside about her research). She also helps organize symposia where other researchers talk. Claudia also represents the center by being a member of various committees. She recently attended a meeting of the

With all these different jobs, Claudia says, "That's what I love about this work—the variety. Whether the task is small or large, all the work is directed at one goal—promoting research and education. The best part is, I get to see the outcome of whatever I do." And the biggest reward about doing a research project is knowing that "once you get the answer to something, you've got it for the first time ever."

The Desert Research Center is in such a remote area that the nearest grocery store is more than 75 miles away. In the summer, Claudia says, she misses ice cream. She also misses going to restaurants and having friends drop by. But people do travel that far—friends, scientists, students—and they usually stay awhile.

In her spare time, Claudia writes songs and paints. She and Jim like to run with their dog Brewer.

Sue Hunter

ASSISTANT CURATOR **of Marine Mammals,**
National Aquarium in Baltimore, MD

Major in Zoology

Assistant Curator
Marine Mammals

Showtime for Dolphins and Seals

At the outdoor seal pool, Sue Hunter isn't the average person watching the feeding session, she's working. She watches the animals that she knows well to check how they are responding to the staff trainers. She checks the staff's narration and showmanship and notes how the audience is attentive and asks questions. She makes a mental note to talk to staff about the harp seal Mack. He was being picked on by a male gray seal and was removed from the pool. She will ask them to make suggestions about when Mack should be returned to the pool.

Sue is the assistant curator of marine mammals. That means she oversees the medical and behavioral status of the seals and dolphins at the Baltimore Aquarium. There are 6 bottlenose dolphins, 2 gray seals, 7 harbor seals, and the harp seal named Mack. Sue also has administrative duties, attends confer-

- Zoo curators entry level $20,000, mid-range $38,000, up to $100,000
Source: Encyclopedia of Careers and Vocational Guidance

In 2nd grade wanted to train killer whales

Took zoology and biology in high school

Worked in kennel

Training sessions are short, maybe 5 minutes, but they are frequent and consistent.

ences, and writes papers for publication. She works closely with the other Aquarium departments like medical, special events, audio visual, and education. But the biggest part of her job is managing and building the team of 11 trainers who work directly with the mammals—setting their goals, improving their training skills, and helping them when needed.

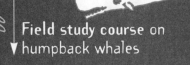

Got lots of experience while earning money for college degree

Field study course on humpback whales

Volunteered, then hired at Baltimore Aquarium

Play and Work Schedules

"**O**ur scheduling of activities and staff work times is quite complex," says Sue. Senior staff plan the daily schedule, which Sue checks and approves. There are from three to seven performances a day, when dolphins and seals show off for the visitors. Not all animals perform in each show, but all animals and staff do a variety of sessions that have to be scheduled. There are learning sessions, play sessions, and the social sessions that build relationships between trainer and animal. "An animal is not going to perform for someone it doesn't know or trust, so social sessions are important." There are also environmental enrichment sessions. "For the dolphins, we provide stuff like a TV in front of a window, ice blocks in the

Married
Chuck

Promoted to
assistant
curator

water, a platform, toys with fish inside, and sprinklers," Sue says.

Sue's job also includes research projects. "We are taking on an environmental enrichment study with the seals. We put novel devices such as a floating platform with artificial 'sea weed' under it, an artificial grass bed, and a tube sculpture with sprinklers in the pool and watch behavior. We compare the behavior with and without the devices. We want to learn what this really does for the animals."

Preparing for the Competition

"When I was in second grade, I was asked what I wanted to be when I grew up and I immediately answered, 'I want to train killer whales.'

I'm not sure where that came from, but it seems like I've always wanted to work with animals."

Growing up in Maryland, Sue had pets and a love for horses. In high school she took zoology and biology because she believed these courses would help her get a job training animals. Sue knew she would face a lot of competition for the limited number of jobs available. She decided to get as much experience as possible. To earn money to start college, Sue worked in a kennel full-time for a year. And she worked all through college, sometimes full-time (it took 6 years). She learned what she liked and didn't like, and her work experience expanded her job opportunities. But she was careful to plan her college courses so if she couldn't work with marine mammals she could go to veterinary school and maybe work with horses.

She Learned from the Birds and the Whales

CAREER CHECKLIST ✓

Over the 6-year period of her schooling, Sue worked with many animals. She worked for the U. S. Fish and Wildlife Service at a wildlife research center caring for birds in the toxicology section. Later she returned to the center and worked with the captive breeding program for rare and endangered birds. She also worked with birds at the University of Maryland. She worked with horses and rode at different stables in the area.

To find out what it was like doing research in the field, Sue took a field study course for college credit and spent 2 months on a boat studying humpback whales. She volunteered at the Baltimore Aquarium for a while caring for fish. She volunteered at the National Zoo in Washington, DC, as a narrator. "They taught us what to say. That was where I learned to talk over a microphone."

That mike experience helped Sue get her first opportunity to train marine mammals. At the job interview with a company that used to give shows all over the United States,

This career is for you if you ...

Are team oriented, get along well with people

Love marine mammals

Are patient

Can be very consistent

Are calm under stress and can think on your feet

Don't mind hard work

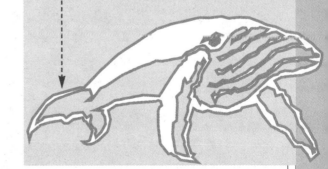

GROUNDBREAKERS

Since receiving her doctorate degree in neurophysiology (nervous system) in 1973, Patricia Brown-Berry has traveled around the world studying bats. She has written about their biology, especially their vocal communications and echolocation. "Bats are dolphin-like with extraordinary navigational systems. They fly in total darkness, sending out high-frequency, high-intensity sounds that bounce back to them on striking objects," she says. Echolocation also informs bats of texture, size, shape, and those insects edible and those not. Often called "the bat lady," she makes every effort to educate people about bats and their importance in the ecosystem. "Bats are said to have rabies, to carry diseases. There are only 10 cases … in all of the U.S. public health records. Household pets are rabid in much greater numbers than bats," she says. She is director of the Maturango Museum (Ridgecrest, Calif.) dedicated to the natural resources of the Mojave Desert.

Source: Los Angeles Times, December 16, 1990.

she had to audition by pretending she was giving a show. Sue landed the job and worked full-time for about 7 months with the dolphin and sea lion shows at Kings Dominion Park near Williamsburg, VA.

One summer a paid position opened up at the Baltimore Aquarium's rain forest section. Sue got the job, partly because of her experience with birds and partly because they knew her from when she had been a "fish" volunteer. During Sue's last year of college, she applied again to the Aquarium, now with her dolphin training experience under her belt. She got a part-time marine mammal trainer position. When she graduated with her degree in zoology, she became a full-time staff trainer.

Seals Her Favorites

Sue worked a lot with the seals exhibit. She wanted to educate people who visited the seals. She worked with other departments to create taped narrations and music that would play when staff weren't at the seal pool. Sue also started the volunteer narrator program, training volunteers to narrate the shows and answer visitor questions so that staff could

concentrate on working with the mammals. She became supervisor of trainers, then was promoted to assistant curator.

What Trainers Do

The trainers' day starts early preparing food and cleaning. This is hard physical work, moving heavy boxes of frozen fish in and out of the freezer, carrying heavy buckets filled with fish, cleaning the kitchen twice a day, cleaning the decks, diving in pools and cleaning the algae. "In a show facility like the Aquarium, trainers are constantly in and out of a wet suit, so it seems you are always wet."

The water must be tested, the animals weighed, and the sessions started. There is always something going on. The day is long, so the trainers work early or late schedules, weekends, and holidays. When there are new animals or ill animals, staff is there all the time to do whatever the animals need.

Training is learned on the job. Biology, zoology, even psychology can teach you a lot about animals in general, but not a lot about training. Sue explains basic training theory as positive reinforcement. "You reinforce the behavior or you are neutral, you aren't negative. The main reinforcement is food, but there are other things that the animal likes. We pet them, rub them; we get excited for them, jump in the water or give them toys."

Trainers use the whistle in training. For example, in dolphin training the whistle lets the dolphin know that it has done the right thing. The reinforcement comes later. You can't really reinforce the dolphin the instant it reaches the top of its jump, but you can blow the whistle then. Trainers begin by teaching the dolphin to touch a target, like a cork at the end of a pole. Once the dolphin learns to do that, the target is moved around to teach other behaviors, and the dolphin learns to follow it. Flips are taught by first getting the dolphin to follow a target under water; then the target is gradually moved into the air. Later, a signal, like a handclap, is taught as the trick is performed and the target is gradually taken away.

Training sessions are short, maybe 5 minutes, but they are frequent and consistent. It takes several months to train one behavior

Trainers are constantly in and out of a wet suit, so it seems you are always wet.

and a lot of patience. Not all behaviors are for an audience. The animals are also trained to cooperate with medical procedures. Once an animal performs a behavior, trainers must continue working with it to maintain that behavior. The shows rarely call for the same behaviors in the same order. It keeps the animals alert to not know what's coming next.

Sue loves her work, and while she is doing less actual training now, she is guiding others to be successful trainers. When Sue is not working, she lives in the countryside near Baltimore. She and her husband, Chuck, met when she was transporting two dolphins from the Aquarium to Sea World in Ohio, where Chuck worked as an animal care specialist. They share their home with dogs, cats, fish, a lizard, and horses. Sue has a pager so she can be contacted if she is needed. It's a long drive in to work, but Sue says it's worth it to be able to have her own horses.

Tonya Williamson

OWNER, Ostrich Farm, La Luz, NM

Ostrich Farmer

Farming is for the Birds

Tonya Williamson lives on the same land that her great grandparents did in La Luz, New Mexico. Tonya is interested in a type of farming her great grandparents never could have imagined—raising ostriches and selling the meat for food and the leather for purses, boots, belts, and hats. There are now almost 2,000 ostrich farms within the United States and Canada. North America is discovering that ostrich is a delicious meat with not much fat and a good alternative to the more traditional turkey, chicken, beef, and pork.

If ostriches aren't sold for meat, they can live for 75 years or more. About 25 of the ostriches on the Williamson farm are breeders. These are the family pets. Many have been around for about 10 years. "I don't allow myself to be affected or get close to the birds that are going to be sold," Tonya says

Owner pays self a salary and profits from the business

TONYA'S CAREER PATH

Grows up on
her family's
farm

Studies math and science at
New Mexico State University

Marries Rick

"The ones that are for breeding are the ones that I can have affection for."

Tonya has been interested in livestock farming since she was a small girl. Her parents raised chickens, and they planted pecan trees that are harvested for their nuts. Tonya always liked the baby animals—horses, chicks, and calves. Today her favorite job is doing the research that allows the farm to produce the baby ostriches with the most meat. That means understanding the optimal time for the egg in the incubator, how much weight loss the egg should have in order to produce a healthy bird, and what the best hatching time is. The information about what procedures produce the best bird is stored on a computer and shared among the ostrich farmers through the Internet and at seminars, so that others can learn from the research.

Begins farming
▼ with Rick

Has daughter
▼ Amber and son Levi

Begins ostrich
▼ farming

Ostriches are Dangerous

The life of the ostrich bred for meat is a short one. Eggs are collected from the hens at the end of the day during the spring, summer, and fall. They are labeled so the eggs from a particular bird can be identified. Ostriches are kept in pens. Tonya has three dogs that help her move ostriches out of the way so she can collect the eggs. The dogs "herd" the ostriches the way sheep dogs herd sheep. Ostriches use their feet to defend themselves, and they can really hurt a person because of the strength of their legs and the way their claws are shaped. It's important that the dogs get them away from the person who is collecting the eggs.

Tonya then takes the eggs to the incubator facility and washes them with a special liquid that will protect them from bacteria. Then the eggs are put in cold storage at 55 degrees

Farming is really great. It has let me stay close to my family, and we all pull together.

so they can lose some weight for a better and healthier chick later on, and eventually moved from there to the incubator. After 42 days Tonya hatches them, using a hammer to break the egg open. The chicks weigh around two pounds when they come out of the egg.

be sold for meat and leather will be taken to a slaughter house 10 to 12 months after they hatch. Their meat is sold to restaurants and grocery stores in the area for such dishes as ostrich burgers and ostrich fajitas. Ostrich tastes something like beef and can be cooked

After 42 days Tonya hatches the egg, using a hammer to break it open. The chicks weigh around two pounds when they come out of the egg.

Baby chicks are then put in a grassy pen separate from their parents, so they won't be trampled. Tonya helps them to learn to eat and drink and watches them grow throughout the year. Those birds that are destined to

in similar ways. But the ostrich is a lean red meat, with less fat than turkey or chicken. Tonya and her family eat it two or three times a day.

The ostrich hides are sent to Baton Rouge,

LA, where they are tanned and dyed, and then returned so they can be sold as leather. The leather of the ostrich is the most sought after in the world for its beauty and durability.

A Family's Business

Tonya's farming work is supported by her entire family—her husband, Rick, and her two children, Amber (19) and Levi (16). Both children are raising their own birds to help finance their college education.

It was Rick's idea to get into ostrich farming. When he sold a lumber business, he was looking for a business to invest in for the long term. Ostriches appealed to him because they provided a new and healthy type of meat, and because the farming would yield money to live on for many years into the future. At first Tonya was skeptical, but now she loves ostrich farming. She likes the fact that she is providing people with another healthy choice for meat. Usually Rick will work the pecan orchards and she and the kids will do the ostrich farming.

"Some years the money from pecans pays our way and other years, it's the birds," she says. "My goal is to raise 30 babies out of every female breeder every year." Right now

CAREER CHECKLIST ✓

This career is for you if you ...

Are interested in producing a new and different food product that is healthy

Like scientific research

Like to do physical work and work outside

Can think like a business person

GROUNDBREAKERS

Since 1983, Terri Crisp has participated in 20 disasters rescuing animals. A volunteer for the Santa Clara (CA) Humane Society, she has rescued animals from floods, fires, and hurricanes.

She became the first volunteer for the United Animal Nation's Emergency Animal Rescue Service Program, and she went to Yellowstone National Park in 1988 to help rescue wild life. When the Exxon oil tanker Valdez went aground, she spent 6 months helping animals during the oil spill cleanup.

For more about her rescue work, read Out of Harm's Way *by Terri Crisp and Samantha Glen, Pocket Books.*

she's making about $100 per bird sold, but that will change as the market for ostrich meat and leather changes.

Tonya's parents live across the road, and they can help out when the Williamsons want to take some vacation time. "Raising ostriches could be a time and one-half job for one person, but with the entire family pitching in, it's not a bad way to make a living," Tonya says.

Tonya's college courses have helped her to raise the birds successfully. She went to college for 3 years at New Mexico State University, where she took lots of courses in math and microbiology in preparation for a career as a dentist. She didn't ever go to dental school, but she uses the science courses in her work with the birds. She uses the math to understand feed ratios and incubation variables. The science is really important to understand the different techniques for incubation and hatching, to understand what problems could be developing, and to solve them before she loses a bird.

To help promote the value of ostrich meat, Tonya gives tours around her farm. More than 1,200 people a year visit her farm to see what ostrich farming is like.

You don't have to know everything. You can mimic others who are doing the farming successfully. For example, I'm not good at mechanical things, but I have others I can call upon to help me. Having a good vet you can count on when you need him or her is really important.

Getting Started on your own Career Path

What to do now

To help you prepare for a career working with animals, the women interviewed for this book recommend things you can do while in middle school, junior high, and high school:

Dee Craig, Small Animal Veterinarian

Courses to take in high school if you are research oriented: Biology, Chemistry, Algebra, Trigonometry, Physics, and Statistics.

Janc Scigler, Horse Farm Owner

Educate yourself and have some type of employment experience outside the horse world. You will need people skills and business skills.

Laura Thompson-Olais, Wildlife Management

Study the sciences—zoology (study of vertebrates and invertebrates), ornithology (study of birds), mammology (study of mammals), and wildlife management.

Lydia Wade, Assistance Dog Trainer

Get active and join groups now, so you will be around people doing something with animals similar to what you are interested in. Then volunteer to help. There are always things to be done that are fun.

Claudia Luke, Zoologist, Herpetologist

Start your study of nature near home with a place that is relatively wild—it could be the nearest park or your back yard. Read field guides and join outdoor groups. Observe and keep notes in a journal describing what you see.

Sue Hunter, Assistant Curator, Marine Mammals

Don't limit yourself to one thing, like marine biology, but get a broad degree that includes some psychology. Seek out internships and field studies that give college credit. Also volunteer, so people get to know you, and join organizations.

Recommended reading

Jane Seigler, Horse Farm Owner
The Pony Club Book. (1995). Boonesboro, MD: Half Halt Press; 64 pp., $19.95.

The Nature of Horses by Stephen Budiansky (1997) New York: The Free Press (Simon and Schuster); 290 pp., $30.00

The Man Who Listens to Horses, an autobiography by Monty Roberts.

The Horse Whisperer by Nicholas Evans. (1995). New York: Delacorte Press. (Also on audio cassettes)

You can get a list of books from Half Halt Press, Boonesboro, MD, also visit your local horse tack stores. There is a huge body of knowledge about horses.

Megan Dudek, Bird Handler/Interpreter
All Creatures Great and Small by James Herriot. (1992). New York: St. Martin's Press.

Claudia Luke, Zoologist, Herpetologist
The Amateur Naturalist by Gerald Durrell. (1989). New York: David McKay Co.

Man Meets Dog by Konrad Z. Lorenz. (1994). New York: Kodanska America

Lydia Wade, Assistance Dog Trainer
First Lady of the Seeing Eye, by Morris Frand and Blake Clark (1957). New York: Hold

References:
Encyclopedia of Career and Vocational Guidance. (1997). Chicago: J. G. Ferguson

Peterson's Scholarships, Grants, and Prizes. (1997). Princeton, NJ: Peterson's.
http://www.petersons.com

Professional Groups

Check these groups for local meetings, conferences, internships, and apprenticeships.

General

Association for Women in Science

Local chapters, mentoring program for college students, scholarships for those in Ph.D. programs.

    1200 New York Ave., Suite 650; Washington, DC 20005

    1-800-886-AWIS; 202 326-8940 (voice); 202 326-8960 (fax)

    awis@awis.org (email)

    http://www.awis.org

Dee Craig, Veterinarian

American Veterinarian Medical Association

    1931 North Meakham Rd., #100, Schaumburg, IL 60173

    (847) 925-8070

American Animal Hospital Association

    P.O. Box 150899, Denver, CO 80215-0899

    (800) 883-6301

Megan Dudek, Bird Handler/Interpreter

International Association of Avian Trainers and Educators (IAATE)

    Minnesota Zoo

    13000 Zoo Blvd., Apple Valley, MN 55124

    (612) 431-9356

American Association of Zoo Keepers

    635 S.W. Gage Blvd., Topeka. KS 66606-2066

    800 242-4519

Shawna Hamann, Exotic Animal Trainer

Moorpark College Teaching Zoo

    7075 Campus Road, Moorpark, CA 93021

    805 378-1441

International Brotherhood of Teamsters

    25 Louisiana Ave, NW, Washington, DC 20001

    202 624-6800

Sue Hunter, Assistant Curator, Marine Mammals
America Zoo and Aquarium Association
  Conservation Center, 7970-D Old Georgetown Rd.
  Bethesda, MD 28814-2493

IAMATA - International Marine Animal Trainers Association
  1200 South Lake Shore Drive, Chicago, IL 60605

Alliance of Marine Mammal Parks & Aquariums
dedicated to conservation through public display; education, and research
  103 Queen Street, Alexandria, VA 22315
  (703) 549-0137

Claudia Luke, Zoologist, Herpetologist
U.S. Fish & Wildlife Service
  1849 C St. NW, Washington, DC 20240
  (202) 208-3100 or (202) 208-5634; personnel office (703) 358-1743

Environmental Protection Agency, Washington, DC
  Public Information (202) 260-2080;
  Web site Http://www.epa.gov

Jane Seigler, Horse Farm Owner
Various organizations devoted to a particular breed of horse.

Women's Professional Rodeo Association
  1235 Lake Plaza Dr. #134, Colorado Springs, CO 80906

Daniela Spigai, Entrepreneur, Pet Sitter and Exerciser
National Association of Professional Pet Sitters
  1200 G St. NW, Washington, DC 20005-4709
  (202) 393-3317 or (800) 296-7387

An Income Of Her Own
  1804 West Burbank Blvd., Burbank, CA 91506-1315
  (800) 350-2978

Laura Thompson-Olais, Wildlife Management
U.S. Fish & Wildlife Service, Division of Refuges
  1849 C St. NW, Washington, DC 20240
  (800) 344-WILD

National Park Service
P.O. Box 37127, Washington, DC 20013
(202) 208- 4747 or (202) 523-5133

Forest Service
P.O. Box 96090, Washington, DC 20090
(202) 285-1760

Lydia Wade, Assistance Dog Trainer
For local volunteer opportunities, check this directory: International Assistance Dog Providers in the U.S. 1995 by Carla Stevenson and Gary Dodson. $27 (includes shipping). Available from:
NC Service Dogs
3598 West Delphi Pike, Marion, IN 46952
(765) 384-5530

Bonita Bergin
The Assistance Dog Institute (TADI)
P.O. Box 2334, Rohnert Park, CA 94927
(707) 585-0300

Delta Society
289 Perimeter Road East, Renton, WA 98055
(425) 226-7357

Assistance Dogs International (610-869 4902, ext 10), - members work to get standards for certification of trainers and dogs, promote safety in public and in homes.

Canine Companions for Independence (707) 577-1700

Tonya Williamson, Ostrich Farmer
American Ostrich Association
3950 Fossil Creek Blvd, #200, Ft. Worth, TX 76137
(817) 232-1200

National 4-H Council
7100 Connecticut Ave., Chevy Chase, MD 20815-4999
(301) 961-2856

Getting training

"Volunteer for what you love to do. When you volunteer in an office or for an organization, you see exactly how things are run. Usually nothing is hidden from you because they need your help. You can find out a lot about the individuals and the job and find out whether or not you are interested in working with them." Laura Thompson-Olais, Wildlife Management

Volunteering is the best way to get practical experience. Also check with your local and state parks, zoos, and aquariums for volunteer and internship programs.

A Good Place to Start to Discover the Internet

More than 700 sites listed here chosen by librarians to help young adults get acquainted with the Internet/World Wide Web. *http://www.ala.org/parentspage/greatsites/*

How COOL Are You?!

Cool girls like to DO things, not just sit around like couch potatoes. There are many things you can get involved in now to benefit your future. Some cool girls even know what careers they want (or think they want).

Not sure what you want to do? That's fine, too... the Cool Careers series can help you explore lots of careers with a number of great, easy to use tools! Learn where to go and to whom you should talk about different careers, as well as books to read and videos to see. Then, you're on the road to cool girl success!

Written especially for girls, this new series tells what it's like today for women in all types of jobs with special emphasis on nontraditional careers for women. The upbeat and informative pages provide answers to questions you want answered, such as:

- ✔ **What jobs do women find meaningful?**
- ✔ **What do women succeed at today?**
- ✔ **How did they prepare for these jobs?**
- ✔ **How did they find their job?**
- ✔ **What are their lives like?**
- ✔ **How do I find out more about this type of work?**

Each book profiles ten women who love their work. These women had dreams, but didn't always know what they wanted to be when they grew up. Zoologist Claudia Luke knew she wanted to work outdoors and that she was interested in animals, but she didn't even know what a zoologist was, much less what they did and how you got to be one. Elizabeth Gruben was going to be a lawyer until she discovered the world of Silicon Valley computers and started her own multimedia company. Mary Beth Quin grew up in Stowe, Vermont, where she skied competitively and taught skiing. Now she runs a ski school at a Virginia ski resort. These three women's stories appear with others in a new series of career books for young readers.

The Cool Careers for Girls series encourages career exploration and broadens girls' career horizons. It shows girls what it takes to succeed, by providing easy-to-read information about careers that young girls may not have considered because they didn't know about them. They learn from women who are in today's workplace—women who know what it takes today to get the job.